Becoming a Millionaire Within a Year With No Effort!

Becoming a Millionaire Within a Year With No effort

John R. Colt

Copyright © 1999, 2000, 2001
All Rights Reserved

Sabongui & Sabongui, Publishers
Montreal, Canada

Becoming a Millionaire Within a Year With No Effort!
Sabongui & Sabongui, Publishers
470 Harris Street
St. Laurent, Quebec   H4N 2H3, Canada

Copyright © 2001
All Rights Reserved

No part of this publication may be reproduced, stored in a retrieval system, or transmitted, in any form or by any means, electronic, mechanical, photocopying, recording, or otherwise without the prior written permission of the publishers.

This manual is sold with the understanding that the publisher and author are not engaged in rendering legal, accounting or other professional advice. If legal or other expert assistance is required, the services of a competent professional should be sought. The author, publisher, distributor, or reseller shall have neither liability nor responsibility to any person or entity with respect to any loss or damage caused, or alleged to have been caused, directly or indirectly, by the information contained in this book.

Sabongui & Sabongui, Publishers
Montreal, Canada

Becoming a Millionaire Within a Year With No Effort!

Dedicated to: Wadid, Leila, Amir, Camille, Patrick, Marie-Marguerite. Love you forever.

Non Illegitimi Carborundum

Becoming a Millionaire Within a Year With No Effort!
Cataloguing in Publication Data

Colt, John R., 1967-

Becoming a millionaire within a year, with no effort

ISBN 0-9686151-0-4

1. Finance, Personal–Psychological aspects. 2. Self-realization. I. Title.

BF637.S8C64 1999   332.024'001'9   C99-901437-4

Becoming a Millionaire Within a Year With No Effort!

Contents
Introduction

Part I - Background
    1. My Story

Part II - The essential Concepts
    2. E-Conomics
    3. E-Volution
    4. E-Motion

Part III- Advanced concepts
    5. The Choice
    6. The River of Time
    7. The Dreamtime
    8. Strength
    9. The Power
    10. Relax
    11. The Will
    12. Effortlessness
    13. Keep your Big Mouth Shut
    14. Resolve
    15. Get Over It
    16. Don't Lose Money
    17. Dis-Stress
    18. The Fundamental Principle
    19. The Dialogue
    20. The Plan

Epilogue- The New Beginning

Becoming a Millionaire Within a Year With No Effort!

Becoming a Millionaire Within a Year With No Effort!

Introduction

> "You must understand that by choosing to fulfill your dream, you are choosing a path that is unique to you."

Introduction

This book is written exclusively for those who wish to be millionaires. If you are not one of those, then stop reading this book and put it down. This book is not for you, as it will not be useful to you, and it will not make sense to you. Just go about doing what you were doing before. You are always welcome to come back and join us when you choose the goal of becoming a millionaire.

If, however, you are a person who has a goal of becoming a millionaire, then I am happy to welcome you. You are about to embark on a journey that will change your life. What you will find contained here is the truth that you have been searching for. Contained in these pages is the inspiration to follow your path. The true nature of happiness and love is here.

You must understand that by choosing to fulfill your dream, you are choosing a path that is unique to you. It is yours alone. You will have to break away from the established mindset of society. It is no longer suitable for you. You have bigger dreams and visions. The attitude of the herd will not be useful to you. If the understanding of the masses were enough, then everyone would be a millionaire. Obviously, they are not. You must consciously remove yourself from their influence on your thinking, before you suffer irreparable damage. You have been lucky to come this far without your brain being completely assimilated. Congratulations.

Being a millionaire is the best possible thing that you can do for society. If you have more, you have more to give. If you are financially independent, then you will not be a financial burden on others. Contrary to what you have been led to believe, your dream of being a millionaire is extremely virtuous. Having the status of a millionaire will give you the influence to make a major difference in the world; it will give you a voice. It is the right thing to do. There are different rules and regulations for millionaires. It is a cut off point for many things, including immigration and investment laws just to name a few.

Being a millionaire will allow you more freedom that mere financial freedom. It is a door that leads to opening yourself up to experiences that until now you have only dreamed of. These experiences are your birthright, though you have been led to believe that you are somehow unworthy.

Consider, for example, the pain that you feel when you pick up a travel magazine and see the beautiful pictures of sunny beaches filled with healthy, happy and attractive people, only to remind yourself that these experiences are not for you, that you are in some way less deserving than the people on the pages of the magazine. My dear friend, I empathize with you completely. I have been there. I feel your

Becoming a Millionaire Within a Year With No Effort!

frustration, and I would spare you further damage to your self-image. You deserve so much more than the meager crumbs that they have thrown you from their table.

My sincere wish is to shine as a beacon in the world, so that I can help restore the vision of those whose lives I touch. What you will find here, you will recognize as true. These are the truths that you knew before your thoughts were contaminated with self-doubt. I feel that I have been truly blessed in my life, and my greatest blessing is that I have the privilege of sharing my joys with others. I am ready now to share with you my technique for generating unlimited abundance in this life. If you are ready to step into more wealth than you have ever dared to dream of, turn the page...

Becoming a Millionaire Within a Year With No Effort!

Becoming a Millionaire Within a Year With No Effort!

My Story

"Believe me, if someone as flawed as me can do it, so can you! I am not different from you, we come from the same mold."

Chapter 1
My Story

So, anyway... here's my story: After finishing College, and spending some time in the army, I decided that I wanted to start everything from scratch and to become a millionaire.

So, I gave away everything that I had, and headed out west with only a dollar in my pocket, determined to make a million dollars by the end of the year. People couldn't believe how foolish I was. But I just kept on going. And therein lies the first lesson. When you choose to follow your own path, people will think you are nuts. You must accept this and go on. It is not enough to think outside the box, you must live outside the box. And sometimes it gets cold out there.

It occurred to me that if I were to invest that dollar rather than spend it, I would then have two dollars. So, I went to the dollar store, and bought an audio tape, and asked my brother to buy it from me. Naturally, he was happy to. Therein lies the second lesson. When you are decided to do something, magic happens, doors open, people help.

It then occurred to me that if I kept on doubling my money with each transaction, I would have $1,000,000 within only 20 transaction! So I wrote this on a sheet of paper, like the one on the next page, that I kept in my pocket:

Becoming a Millionaire Within a Year With No Effort!

My Million Dollar Project:

Amount	Date	Item
1. $2		
2. $4		
3. $8		
4. $16		
5. $32		
6. $64		
7. $128		
8. $256		
9. $512		
10. $1,000		
11. $2,000		
12. $4,000		
13. $8,000		
14. $16,000		
15. $32,000		
16. $64,000		
17. $128,000		
18. $256,000		
19. $512,000		
20. ONE MILLION DOLLARS		

Becoming a Millionaire Within a Year With No Effort!

And therein lies the third lesson: Make a map and follow it.

So, I decided to test my theory. I looked around for things that people really wanted, and then I supplied it to them. For example, I went to the park on a hot summer day and noticed that people were hot and probably thirsty. So I went over to the corner store, and bought some cans of soft drinks for 50 cents each and sold them for a dollar each. That was simple enough. So I did it over and over again, doubling my money each time. So in one day, I was able to take my $2 and turn them into $32. Do you think that this is really difficult to do? Not at all! Therein lies the fourth lesson: find something that people want and give it to them. Just give the people what they want.

I then went to local pawnshops and looked for something for my $32 that I could sell for twice what I paid. I have a pretty good knowledge of musical instruments, and I was able to identify a guitar (A real cheap one) that I could double my money on. Then I hit on a plan: Why don't I use this to produce income instead? So I stood on the street corner and played that guitar all day, until I had $64, and then I took it back to the pawnbroker, explaining that I had changed my mind. So, I didn't even have to look for a buyer! Herein lies the fifth lesson: Stay flexible. Don't get stuck on an idea!

By the time I got to the Rocky Mountains, it was ski season. I had $64 in my pocket, and I didn't want to spend it, as this was the money that I was going to use to become a

Becoming a Millionaire Within a Year With No Effort!

millionaire, so I got a job working on a ski hill. Herein lies the sixth lesson: Don't confuse your bread and butter with your cash cow. Make sure that you have an income to spend on living expenses, so that you don't have to spend your fortune on food and shelter.

The first thing that I did upon getting the job was to throw a Chicken-wing party for my colleagues. As you may have guessed, I bought $64 worth of party food and drinks, and my friends were more than happy to chip in, for a total of $128. Therein lies the seventh lesson: Don't overlook the obvious. You are not proving that you are a genius, just trying to become a millionaire!

At the ski hill that I was working at, there were a lot of Japanese tourists, and none of the staff spoke Japanese. I asked around with the people I worked with, and many of them said they would be interested in taking learning to speak japans, in order to communicate better with the guests. I saw an immediate opportunity, and I went to see the general manager of the ski hill. I told him that I would be happy to organize language lessons for the staff, if he would provide a conference room I the hotel, and help pay for the cost of the teacher. This was a win/win situation for everyone involved, (Which is the only kind of transaction that I would ever become involved in). Everybody wins: the teacher, the staff, the company, the tourists, and ME! Of course, I paid the teacher half of everything that came in, and I was able to double my money on this project. Here is your lesson: make certain everyone wins in the process, you will be able to sleep

Becoming a Millionaire Within a Year With No Effort!

better at night, and you will feel a much greater sense of satisfaction, and you will be able to look people in the eye.

At this time I began to attend auctions. I checked out every kind of auctions there was and discovered that some were better suited to buying and others were better suited to selling. At some auctions, I was the only bidder. Here I was able to find incredible deals. I was able to buy computers for less than $1 and sell them for upwards of $100. All this just by looking for the opportunity, and that is the Eighth lesson: Dig, dig, dig everywhere for opportunities. Follow every hunch, you don't know where each path will lead, but you will learn something every time, and sooner or later, you will spot a perfect deal.

The items that I bought at auction, I sold through the classified ads in my local paper. I took this paper with me everywhere I went, and I consulted it before every auction. Before I bought anything, I would always open the paper to check if I would be able to sell my item at twice what it cost me. One day, as I looked through the paper, I noticed that there was an ad in the *Items Wanted* section in which someone was looking for a specific type of synthesizer. Two columns over, on the same page, of the same paper, another person was selling the exact make and model of instrument that the buyer wanted. I called them both up, and was able to sell make both the transactions that afternoon. It would have been a simple matter for either party in the transactions to open the paper and find the opportunity themselves, but everyone has a limited amount of time each day, and can't do

Becoming a Millionaire Within a Year With No Effort!

everything. Luck seems to come your way when you are actively engaged in seeking out opportunities! And here is the tenth lesson: Look for a hole in the market, a discrepancy between the selling price and the buying price that already exist in the market place. You don't have to create conditions, just exploit them.

    With this in mind, I started checking out the Internet as a source for opportunities. I was interested in high end watches, so just for fun, I placed an ad on an online auction, saying that I was looking for a specific type of watch, and that I was willing to pay up to $1000 for it. Eventually, I was contacted by a seller, and made the deal. I immediately posted this item up on the same auction board where I had bought it for $2,000. Guess what? It sold! I couldn't believe how fortunate I was, but I came to realize that the market is full of these opportunities every single day, and we just don't take advantage of them like we could. As a player on the marketplace, you are providing a valuable service. You are helping people on the one hand dispose of something that they do not want, while providing things for people that do want them. In a sense, you are a broker, and your margin of profit is 50%, and you are worth every penny of that money for the service you are providing. Remember this lesson: Feel good about the service you are providing.

    With the money that I had accumulated, I began attending car auctions. Again, some were good, some were bad, and some were filled with sharks. I learned that the auctions that were run by bailiffs were the ones where I could

Becoming a Millionaire Within a Year With No Effort!

get the best deals. I always had the morning paper with me, since I know nothing about the value of cars. I realized here that I may have to get some repairs done to some of the cars that I was buying, and since I am not a mechanic, I would have to pay for these, and this money would have to be factored in to the price that I would pay. Furthermore, I reasoned, some of the cars that bought would end up being hopeless, and I would have to sell them for scrap. By being careful I was able to grow my assets to tens of thousands of dollars. Here is the lesson you can take with you this time: Cover your ASSets. Don't expose yourself to unnecessary risks, and make sure you have an exit plan. In short, don't do anything stupid.

From here, I got involved in an Internet business start-up, and after I built the company into a going venture, the shares naturally doubled in value. Here is your lesson: Learn to create value. Nothing is valuable until someone gives it value, and that person is you.

Once I had learned this lesson, it was easy to repeat the process a few times, until I had a net worth of one million dollars. Keep this in mind: with every step you take, you will learn more, and it will become easier as you gain confidence and skill.

Believe me, if I could do it, so can you! It is not necessary for you to follow in my footsteps, and do all of the exact things that I did, but rather, get out there and seek your own opportunities. The market is changing each and every

Becoming a Millionaire Within a Year With No Effort!

day, and what works one day, may change the next. Keep you eyes open and follow your own path.

Becoming a Millionaire Within a Year With No Effort!

E-Conomics

"Anyone can dismiss ideas as simple, but it takes a special person to take a simple idea and make it work. Which type of person are you? Are you a person who looks for flaws or opportunities?"

Chapter 2
E-Conomics

Money doesn't exist. It is a figment. It is an invention. The traditional economic model is based on an outmoded set of assumptions that just don't hold up in today's world. It doesn't make sense. If you are to take control of your own financial future, you must learn to look at money in a different way.

For starters, traditional economics assumes scarcity. This is one of the fundamental tents. Economists assume that there is not enough stuff in the world. But, look around you! There is more than enough. There is a condition of abundance, not lack. It is an established fact that we have more than enough food to feed everyone, yet children die each day of starvation, while we dump milk and burn wheat, to control market prices. It is not a problem of creating more it is a question of distribution.

We burn up our atmosphere and ozone, and we destroy the very earth that sustains us in the name of a healthy "economy". Tell me, how healthy is an economy that destroys its own habitat? Clearly the thinking behind these egregious actions is flawed.

All economic theories fall sooner or later. Before the world wars, governments tired to maintain stable currencies.

Becoming a Millionaire Within a Year With No Effort!

Despite their best efforts, , money stubbornly refused to obey, and people began trading currencies at levels that were not planned by any government.

How much money is there in the world, it is impossible to say with any degree of accuracy.

Within this framework, money does not have a stable definition. Rather than one definition of money, there are several. Often, we speak of levels of money. Economists define money as in terms of levels M1, M2, M3, etc... Some forms are considered closer to being cash money, and other forms are considered near-money. Depending on whom you talk to and what the objective is, not everyone will agree on what a given amount of money represents.

These levels of money represent levels of reality. They depend on how many people agree with your definition of money. If you have several people tally up your assets, there is a good chance that no two of them will come up with the same figure.

As you move towards becoming a millionaire, one thing will become clear: you are the one who decides how much you are worth. It is not a question of piling up a million dollars, but rather declaring that you have a net worth of one million dollars and then setting out to prove it. As more and more people (i.e. your banker) agree with you, you will be moving your Millionairedom from the world of imagination to the world of reality.

You have often heard the expression that your first million is the hardest to make. Why is that? It is not because

Becoming a Millionaire Within a Year With No Effort!

it is harder to amass the first million; it is because there is a clear paradigm shift. One day, you just think differently. A light bulb goes off. Bang! I am the one who determines my net worth. Once you have decided that, it is then only a matter of providing supporting arguments to the fact that you are a millionaire.

As we move through this book, please keep an open mind. Becoming a millionaire entrepreneur is not what you thought originally. It is not a question of setting aside a certain amount of money. It is not even a matter of running a successful business. It is a matter of understanding and applying a few basic and fundamental principles. And they are all here. Modify them if you wish, but open your mind. If you go into this trying to judge or trying to examine things, you will get nowhere. You are dead in the water. If you truly want it, the answers are here. If you don't see them the first time, read the book again. It will become clear. This book is concise for a reason: Do you realize that less than 10% of people who buy books actually read them? I have no interest in bogging you down with zillions of technical details. I want you to become a millionaire, and that means that I want you out of these pages and onto your project as soon as possible. I really believe that society would be better if more people were financially independent. And that is what I want for you!

But, don't let the shortness of the chapters, or the deceptively simple ideas, fool you. This is powerful stuff, and it works. There is no doubt about that. There are countless examples of people who have applied these principles,

Becoming a Millionaire Within a Year With No Effort!

including myself. What we are aiming for here is depth rather than breadth, quality rather than quantity.

And when you recognize the truths contained here, act on them. Anyone can dismiss ideas as simple, but it takes a special person to take a simple idea and make it work. Which type of person are you? Are you a person who looks for flaws or opportunities?

Becoming a Millionaire Within a Year With No Effort!

E-Volution

"Your supply of money is never static. It is always in flux. It is always either growing or it is shrinking."

Chapter 3
E-Volution

Growth. Your supply of money is never static. It is always in flux. It is always either growing or it is shrinking. What is your money doing right now? Everything alive starts small and grows exponentially. It is the way of nature. Were you to observe a tree, you would see the exponential growth that it undergoes. Now, this is the case with money. Many people believe that you can save your way to a million dollars. And this may be true, but for the average person, this will take a very long time. Almost certainly more than a year. To make a million dollars in a year requires something else all together. It requires having your money grow at a rapid rate.

Here, we must make the difference between earning money and making money. You earn money by what is know as "working". "Earning" money is what you do when you trade hours of your life for money. The problem is that you have a limited number of hours in a day, which you can sell for money. "Making" money is something else altogether.

There are two ways to make money. First, you can make money when you create it. You are not getting it from someone else. You are the originator of it. You make money the way one would make a clay pot. At first there was no clay

Becoming a Millionaire Within a Year With No Effort!

pot, and then someone made it from scratch. Money can be created the same way. In fact, it is done every day.

This process is surprisingly simple. The essential principle to understand here is that ==the value of money is not fixed. It is constantly changing. A dollar is not an object, it is a unit of measurement.== So, you can never really have a million dollars. You can only have possessions evaluated at one a value of one million dollars. This is a critical distinction. When you hold a dollar bill, what you are holding is a bank note that says that the central bank recognizes that you are entitled to one dollar's worth of products or services by trading that note. A dollar bill is not a dollar.

How can you use this information to become a millionaire? This process can be deceptively simple. Think about how the big financial institutions create their own value. How is the size of a bank measured? Normally, a bank is valued by the amount of deposits that they have on their books. Suppose, for example that a bank has only $1 in deposits. Now, if it lends this money out, then they actually have nothing in the safe out back, but they still have $1 in deposits. Now, suppose further that the person who borrows this money deposits it in the same bank from which he borrowed it. How much does the bank have in deposits? The bank now has $2 in deposits, but if you were to ask them to show you these two dollars, they couldn't. They could only show you $1. If this process continues, the bank could keep lending out the same dollar a million times, and show one

Becoming a Millionaire Within a Year With No Effort!

million dollars worth of deposits in their books. They have created money out of thin air.

Why can the banks do it, and not you? What is the difference? The bank is owned by entrepreneurs, just like yourself. Only they have decided to take control of the amount of money that they have in their lives, and acted on that decision. You can do the exact same thing that they have.

Let us look at some of the wealthiest people in the world, such as Bill Gates. How did they create their money? Did they go and get the money from someone else? No, they also "made" money. They did not earn it. They created it.

How? Well, this type of entrepreneur made their money "on paper". That means that they don't actually have wheelbarrows full of billions of dollars. Rather, what they have is stocks in corporations, and this stock is evaluated at a certain value.

Who decides what the stock is valued at? Well, a stock is simply worth what people are willing to pay for it. Once again, why can the richest men in the world create money in this way, and not you? There is no reason other than the fact that they made a decision and then imposed their will on the world.

How is a stock valued? The market decides. This means that a share is treated just like any other commodity for sale in the marketplace. Any commodity is worth what people pay for it. Let me give you an illustration: if I have a stock of one million pens in a warehouse, and someone buys one pen from me for one penny, how much is my inventory

Becoming a Millionaire Within a Year With No Effort!

of pens worth? It would be worth $10,000. If however, someone buys a pen from me for $1, my inventory is then worth $1 Million Dollars. Since a share is no different from any other commodity, it will be treated exactly the same way. If someone buys one share form my company for $1, and I have one million shares outstanding, how much is my company worth? My company is then worth one million dollars.

So, what do you think? Is it possible for you to be a millionaire within a year? That is too long. You could be a millionaire tomorrow morning, by opening a corporation, issuing one million shares and selling one share for one dollar to someone you know. This is the way that many large corporations get started. In fact, when you read about mergers and acquisitions, much of the time no actual money has changed hands.

Many large corporate takeovers have been financed through stock for stock buyouts. This means that one or both corporations have created and issued stock out of thin air, and traded it for stock, which was also created out of thin air. The value of the companies has gone up simply because they have agreed on a new value.

This information alone can make you a millionaire right now. But we are just getting warmed up. We have a lot more ground to cover. I hope that you are as excited as I am to get started on your journey to becoming a millionaire!

Becoming a Millionaire Within a Year With No Effort!

E-Motion

" Each time a Unit of E-Motion attaches itself to an idea, the vibration of this image is amplified a little bit more until it reaches a critical mass."

Chapter 4
E-Motion

We have determined our direction and implanted firmly in our subconscious the image of ourselves as Millionaires. Now what? The next step is to act on the intuitions that we receive, (By asking "What is the fastest and easiest way to reach my goal of becoming a millionaire?").

You will definitely receive answers to this question. They will either be fragmented or complete. In the first case, you will have only glimpses of what you should do next. In the second case, you will have a complete picture of a complete project. In either case, you will have to begin by taking a single small step.

The fact is, YOU CAN ONLY DO ONE THING AT A TIME. Think about this for a moment. Can you be in two places at once? Hardly, unless you have the gift of ubiquity and omnipresence, in which case you really have any use for a million dollars. Your physical presence exists in a single point in the time-space continuum. This means that you only have one set of tools with which to work. One set of senses, one set of hands, one Central Processing Computer. The machinery that you use to complete a task can only process one set of information at a time. It can only act on one set of instructions from you at a time.

What do we mean when we say, "At a Time"? What is "A Time"? The unit of Time is something that we call a perceptual moment. As we know through science, matter is really energy vibrating at a certain frequency. The key to existence is vibration. You exist as an Alternating Current. Your life energy occurs in pulses. For example, your eyes perceive at somewhere around 30 cycles per second. What seems to be continuous is really a staccato series of images. This is the way that your senses operate. Your central processing computer scans your thoughts and your perceptions a certain number of times per second. Only one of these can enter your consciousness "At a Time". In the same way, your life energy can only be directed towards one goal or action "At a Time", in each perceptual moment.

How do you select what will enter your consciousness in a perceptual moment? This is where E-MOTION comes in. (E-motion is E-nergy translated into -Motion.) E-Motion is the amplification of vibration until it causes motion in the body. In each perceptual moment, one unit of E-Motion is released. This unit of E-Motion attaches itself to the image or idea that is in your Central Processing Computer at the time. It can only attach itself to one unit idea. Each time a Unit of E-Motion attaches itself to an idea, the vibration of this image is amplified a little bit more until it reaches a critical mass. At that point, it will propel you into action and eventually result in bringing the material version of the image into your life.

Becoming a Millionaire Within a Year With No Effort!

Let us say, for example, you see a house that pleases you. In that first perception, the image passes through your Central Processing Computer, and is registered in your memory. It also receives a charge in the amount of one Unit of E-Motion. The second time you see the house; a second Unit of E-Motion is added. Then, as the image of the house is recalled from your memory during the course of your normal days, additional Units are added. At some point, as the emotional charge increases, you wonder about the cost of that house, and if you can afford it. If this continues, the eventual outcome is that you will take concrete steps to acquire this house or its equivalent. You may even obtain it if you keep adding Units of E-Motion by holding the image in your mind.

This is exactly the same as with bringing a MILLION DOLLARS into your life. Every time that you bring the image of yourself as a millionaire into your mind, an additional Unit of E-Motion will be added to it. Eventually, the emotional charge on the image will reach a critical mass, and will propel you to act in the most effective and efficient way, to bring this image of yourself as a millionaire into the present material world.

Do you have a clear image of yourself as a Millionaire? What do you look like? What are you wearing? How do you talk? Who are you with? What do you do with your days? What do you read? What are your hobbies? Ask as many questions as you can, and get a very clear image of your Millionaire Self. Make this image as clear as possible. The

Becoming a Millionaire Within a Year With No Effort!
more that you hold this image in your mind, the closer you are to making it a reality in the material plane.

Becoming a Millionaire Within a Year With No Effort!

The Choice

Becoming a Millionaire Within a Year With No Effort!

"IT IS IMPOSSIBLE TO BREAK THE LAWS OF NATURE!"

Chapter 5
The Choice

The first step in becoming a millionaire is to realize that it is a Choice. That means that it is up to YOU and no one else to choose to create that condition in your life, just as YOU have chosen almost every single condition in your life up to this point.

Think about it. Think about all of the things in your life right now. Think of the things YOU like and the things that YOU don't like. How did YOU get there? How do YOU like your job? Who chose it? Are YOU in a bad relationship? Who chose it? Did YOU choose these things? Did someone else choose them? If so, why are you keeping these things in your life? If there is something in your life right now that you don't like, why are you keeping it in your life? Why don't you get out of it? If you choose not to change it, YOU are choosing to keep it!

Right now, think of something in your life that you like, anything at all. Now, think about how it got there. Think about what you did to bring this condition into your own life. Think about what you did proactively to make it happen. Think about how you responded to the opportunity when it presented itself. Did you recognize it and choose it? Did you take steps to make it happen? Every day that this condition is in your life, you are choosing to keep it there. When you don't want this thing in your life, then you can just let it go. Then, it will no longer be part of your life.

Now, think about something in your life that you don't like. Go through the same thought process. How did this condition get there? Did you choose it? Did you accept it? Is there something about it that you can do, but you are not doing? Why are you keeping this in your life?

Naturally, there are some limits, which help us to learn the natural laws. These laws can work for us or against us. Which would you rather? Try to work with them or try to work against them? If you try to work against them, they can destroy you. IT IS IMPOSSIBLE TO BREAK THE LAWS OF NATURE!

If you work with them, you can choose anything that is in harmony with these natural laws. Have no doubt as to the truth of this statement. Read this again and burn it into your brain:

YOU CAN CHOOSE ANYTHING THAT IS IN HARMONY WITH NATURAL LAWS!

Being a millionaire is within the laws of nature. It is your choice! What will YOU do? Do YOU choose to be a millionaire or do YOU not? YOU make the choice right now, before YOU choose to turn the page.

Becoming a Millionaire Within a Year With No Effort!

The River of Time

"All you have to do is to listen inside you, and the direction will be clear."

Chapter 6
The River of Time

The question is not whether you will be a millionaire or not, the question is: How soon will you succeed at becoming a millionaire? It is a fact that if it is your sincere wish to become a millionaire, you will achieve it. It is a matter of making it happen faster.

Think of the events that occur in time as a flowing river. Let us suppose that your goal is to swim a mile. How fast can you swim this mile? The answer is simple: It depends. It depends on whether you are flowing with the current or against it, and how fast that current is flowing. Using natural laws to become a millionaire is exactly the same. If you are trying to swim against the stream of natural law, then you may never reach your goal. If however, you swim with the stream, there is no problem. You may have to make no effort at all, and you will reach your goal.

So, in order for you to become a millionaire in the shortest amount of time possible, it is helpful to examine how to get into the stream and flow with it. The beauty of it is that you already have access to this understanding within you. It is right there where you need it. All you have to do is to listen inside you, and the direction will be clear. It is quite a simple process, really. Ask your internal guidance system what

Becoming a Millionaire Within a Year With No Effort!

is the fastest and easiest way for you to become a millionaire, and then wait for the answer. This system is really amazing, and it works. You don't have to be any kind of spiritual wizard or anything. All that you have to do is to ask, and the answer will be provided. You do not need to make any conscious efforts at resolving the issue. Just relax and go about what you do, and the answer will appear.

My experience with this has been extremely profitable. You can get the answers to any kind of question, whether it is simple or complicated, important or trivial. And, YOU DON'T HAVE TO MAKE ANY EFFORT!

When is the best time to do this? Just before falling asleep. Whether it is for the night or just for a nap, often you wake up with the answer. Other times, you wake up with a clue as to where to find the answer. There will, however, always be a reply to your request. Sometimes you may not recognize it. Or, you may forget that you asked a question, but rest assured that the answer has been provided.

So, tonight, before going to sleep, ask yourself the question: **WHAT IS THE SIMPLEST AND FASTEST WAY FOR ME TO BECOME A MILLIONAIRE WITHIN A YEAR?** The answer to this question will be provided for you, with no effort, upon awakening. You don't even have to trust this method for it to work. If you want the answer, **JUST ASK THE QUESTION!**

Becoming a Millionaire Within a Year With No Effort!

The Dreamtime

"What you think about will come about."

Chapter 7
The Dreamtime

All life begins as a dream. The matter that you believe that you see is really not matter at all. The matter that you see is really made up of particles, and these particles in turn are nothing more than energy. Energy is a form of vibration. There is only one kind of vibration. It can exist as sound, light, electricity, energy or matter. Your thoughts are vibration.

Your thoughts are therefore no different from matter. Once a thought occurs, it is only a question of time before it will become matter. Of this, however, you can be certain. Once a vibration takes place in the thoughts of a person, it will absolutely take form in the material world. And this will happen whether or not you make a conscious effort to direct your thoughts.

Thus, what you think about will come about. Would you rather have wealth or poverty? Would you rather therefore think about wealth or poverty? Be certain, what you hold as an idea will come into your life. If you want to be a millionaire, what thought should you hold in your mind? The though of being a millionaire! If you have already pictured yourself as a millionaire, that vibration has already been set up, and it will take place. You already exist as you have

Becoming a Millionaire Within a Year With No Effort!

pictured yourself, and the two images you have of yourself are only separated by time. Therefore, you already exist as a millionaire.

YOU ARE ALREADY A MILLIONAIRE! Read that sentence again. Read that sentence again. Read it until you understand it. Once you understand it, you will believe it, because in a very real sense, it is true. It makes sense.

Our concern then, is not so much with creating your wealth, since your wealth already exists. Our concern is with accelerating the process of bringing your wealth into your world. Our concern is with collapsing time, so that it folds over onto itself and creates the circumstances in which your image of yourself as a millionaire comes into being in a short amount of time.

This is much simpler than it sounds. Let us look at the concept of time. There is a way of controlling your relationship with time. I do not need to convince you that we experience the passage of time differently in different circumstances. Sometimes it seems to go faster, and sometimes slower. This is because it not only seems that way; it actually is faster or slower. This has been shown scientifically, by comparing the times of clocks in outer space and at sea level. Time is slower in outer space. Similarly, when you sleep, the passage of time is irrelevant. That is because you are outside of time.

Your perception of time is related to the level of your vibrations. The vibrations of your thoughts depend on the energy, which you put into your thoughts. Now, how can

Becoming a Millionaire Within a Year With No Effort!

you increase the energy, which you put into your thoughts? Simple. By reducing the effort that you put into reaching your goal.

As a living being, you are alive with energy. There is electricity in your nervous system and your heart, your brain is emitting alpha waves, and you are pulsating with chemical reactions creating heat and a form of combustion. You are on fire! You are energy! Every moment, this energy is released into your system. This energy needs an outlet. It gets directed automatically without your participation. It is directed to your beating heart, your breathing, and all of your life functions, including healing and creation. To engage the creation process, this energy is directed toward the images in your subconscious mind, without your effort. The images in your subconscious, which are stored as a form of electro-magnetic vibration, are AMPLIFIED by the energies released into your system. Your subconscious mind establishes the path of least resistance for bringing about the dominant image held in there, and will program your actions for maximum effect and efficiency. You WILL receive the proper instructions of what your actions must be, along with the energy you need to do these actions. What you must do is GET OUT OF THE WAY. You will feel a natural urge to do what must be done. Do not try to control these urges or organize or direct them. If you cooperate, they will bring you to the fulfillment of your desire. Any effort on your part only slows the process, and damages the cybernetic system.

Becoming a Millionaire Within a Year With No Effort!

So, the main preoccupation of someone who wishes to become a millionaire rapidly is to place the image of themselves as a millionaire as the foremost image in their mind. The best time to do this is when the resistance of the conscious mind is at its lowest point, and that is at outskirts of sleep. So, the fastest way of becoming a millionaire is to hold the image of yourself as a millionaire as you are falling asleep, and as you are waking up. It is that simple.

When you are asleep, you are in what is known, in the spirituality of North American Natives, as "The DREAMTIME". When you are in the Dreamtime, you are outside of normal time and from this place, you can manipulate and collapse time, so that you can bring an image from your future into the present. Take advantage of this dreamtime tonight. Picture yourself as a millionaire as you are falling asleep.

Becoming a Millionaire Within a Year With No Effort!

The Strength

Becoming a Millionaire Within a Year With No Effort!

"Stand up! Claim your due! Seize it."

Chapter 8
The Strength

What to do next: Relax. Meditate. Run every morning. Get strong physically. Martial arts. Yoga. Whatever. Get fit. Really fit. Get in the best shape of your life. This is the way. If you are to follow your path, you must heal yourself. You have let yourself get weak. As you get strong, your life energy will increase. This will increase the vibrations of your existence. Your thoughts will begin to materialize instantly. Once this happens, you must be ready to take control of the new situations that you place in your life. If you are weak, you will cry and be crushed. You will whither into despondency and become a shell of a man. Stand up! Cry out! You can do nothing if you are weak. You will do wonders when you are strong.

Remember, you have chosen this condition. You have allowed yourself to become a weakling, because you thought that it was the right thing to do. You have allowed yourself to whither, because you thought that this is what the world wanted. You felt that if you just pleased everybody in the world by doing their bidding and submitting to their whims, you would be saved and they would give you what you wanted. How did that work out for you? Did you get what you were after? How did the world respond to your kindness and your generosity? Did it give you what you wanted? Was your loyalty repaid? Was your service appreciated? Did they give you your due?

The fact is that the world is preoccupied. They don't have time for you. The world will not do your work even if you do its work. The world will not pay your bills even if you paid the world's bills. You must show concern and respect for yourself if you want the world to do the same. If it is money you want, it is money you will get. If you stand up and demand your due, you will receive it. The world will part like the sea. People will get out of your way. If you are fit to receive your due, you will get it with no resistance from the world which once ignored you. The doors that once closed will open up again.

Stand up! Claim your due! Seize it. Take it and exclaim: "This is mine and I am taking it." Offer no explanations or apologies. Take what is yours. There are no excuses. If you are strong enough, you will be ready for opportunity when it presents itself. There can be nothing to stop you. You will be an unstoppable force. You will be an immovable object. When you feel the strength in your shoulders and the power in your legs, you will feel prepared for any challenge that presents itself. You will have the energy to do what needs to be done. You will take what is yours. You will have your MILLION DOLLARS. Accept it and take responsibility for it in no uncertain terms. Clench your fist and say: "This is mine!"

Becoming a Millionaire Within a Year With No Effort!

The Power

"If you are powerful enough to choose life and sustain a living being, are you not powerful enough to cause mere dollars to come into your world?"

Chapter 9
The Power

YOU can do it. You must more than believe this; you must know this. Beyond the shadow of a doubt! There can be no doubt. It is a fact that every thought that you hold in your mind manifests itself in the physical world. Of this there can be no doubt. This is as true for you as it is for anyone else. How do you know this to be true? Look around you. Everything that man has created was once only an idea. The building you are this in. This book. The clothes you are wearing. All of these began in the mind of a person, were mixed with E-Motion (Energy in Motion), were acted upon, and were created. Man is creator. Know this to be true.

"But, I am nothing", you squeal. "I have not done all of these things", you whine. "Someone else did", you complain.

But you are wrong. You have chosen and brought these things into your environment. They are in your world because you have participated in their creative manifestation. They continue to exist, in part because of your investment in their continued existence. Without your participation, they would surely return to the chaos from whence they came. All things that exist now will one day pass and disappear, to return in another form, at another time. The form they take on will again originate in an idea. Make it your idea.

This is Gravity. Scientists are now working on a Unified field theory, which will bring together the concepts that we have of the different forces of the universe. Scientists recognize that there is only one force binding the universe together. This is attraction. This force holds atoms together, planets are kept in orbit, and you are kept on the planet's surface. Can you deny that gravity holds you to the Earth?

Why are you on the Earth and not on a rubber ball? Because the earth has more mass! More mass means more gravitational force. So it is with your dream as well. We know that at a subatomic level, matter is no more than energy that is bound together. This is how mass begins. Your thought is energy. (This is scientific fact; alpha and other waves can be measured in your brain, and are partly electro-magnetic in nature.)

Your thoughts are as seeds. Consider the seed that is planted in the ground. In the seed is contained an idea of the plant that is to grow. Does the plant begin at its full size and mass? No. Over Time, this Idea attracts to it the physical elements with which it will create the physical body of the plant, by using the energy available to it, to increase in mass.

So it is with you. You began as a seed. You were one cell, and through effort, you became two cells, then four, then eight. Today, you have attracted sufficient mass for a fully-grown body, and you continue to replace portions of mass and create energy each moment of each day. YOU have done this. Can you deny that you have existence? Can you deny that you ARE? NO! There is no doubt that you exist and that you have a body that you participated in creating. There is no doubt that you have surrounded yourself with an environment that you continue to choose.

If you have created and chosen all this, can you not now, if you choose, bring any amount of money into your environment? If you are powerful enough to choose life and sustain a living being, are you not powerful enough to cause mere dollars to come into your world?

How much more powerful you are than you have been led to believe! You have been deceived. You have been fooled by your own choice. You have allowed your mind to be manipulated. You have accepted the idea that you are weak and insignificant.

Rest assured, this is not YOUR idea. You have adopted this idea from others. You have accepted thoughts that are not your own. Others have given you this meager impression of yourself, out of ignorance and fear. They have forgotten their nature and their awesome power, and have led you to believe the same.

Think back. YOU have not always believed this. There was a time when you felt invincible. There was a time when you believed that you could do anything. There was a time when you intuitively understood your power, and the infinite possibilities of the universe. You CREATED. You had no fear. YOU had access to all of the knowledge of the universe.

Think! Go back! Reach deep inside you for these memories! There is energy stored within them! They are tightly repressed and bound up. Release them now! They are stored as tightly as neutrons and protons, and contain enough energy to cause a nuclear explosion. Release this energy. It is yours to command. YOU are invincible with this energy. These are the seeds that you need to attract the matter that you desire to have in your world. Be strong. YOU will attract first one atom, then two, then four. And behold, the thought that you held in your mind will have become a reality.

And you will have become a shining example to those who told you that you were weak. And they will see your glory and they will be confounded. But you will not break, because you will have known your awesome power. How simple a matter, then, will it be for you to become a mere millionaire. You are in fact capable of so much more!

Relax

"Do not question your decision. Remain firm in your resolve. Do not budge an inch. Do not compromise. Do not settle."

Chapter 10
Relax

That's right; RELAX. There is no way you can fail. The outcome that you choose will come to pass. The only way that you can fail is by choosing failure. This is indecision. This is vacillation. If you vacillate in your resolve, you are setting up unpredictable vibrations, that may result in anything at all, or nothing at all.

Once having chosen, therefore, relax. Do not second-guess yourself. Do not question your decision. Remain firm in your resolve. Do not budge an inch. Do not compromise. Do not settle for anything less than 100% of your dream. Do not settle for anything less than complete success. Do not settle for anything less than ONE MILLION DOLLARS IN CASH. If that is the decision you've made, then stand your ground. Do not get wishy-washy. Do not become indecisive. It is unbecoming (Un- Becoming: That is, it will not help you to become what you want to become). Do not whine or beg. Stand up, and claim it.

When I say that you should relax, I mean that. Relax your body, relax your mind and relax your heart. Release the tensions that you have in your body. You no longer need to run around like a chicken with your head cut off. Stop. Stop dead in your tracks. You have made your decision; there is nothing more that you need to do. There is no work to be done, save in your own mind. And that work consists of removing all traces of indecision as to what want. Relax.

Relax your mind. You do not need to make any mental effort. You do not need to ask yourself constantly how you will achieve your goal. You do not need to ask yourself over and over again what you must do to achieve your goal. Here is the paradox: Once you let go trying to figure out rationally how you will achieve your goal, your path will be made clear to you, intuitively.

Think of it this way: if you were driving somewhere, and you got lost, you would have two choices: You could keep driving around in circles, or you could stop, take your bearings and ask for directions. But, in order to ask for directions, you must stop.

So it is with your goal of achieving Millionairedom. You must stop what you are doing, and ask your highest Self for directions. It will respond, in a much more natural joyful way than you are now experiencing. In order to ask for directions, you must stop. Relax.

Finally, you must relax your heart. Your heart is the seat of your emotions of fear and desire. Feel this place now. Feel the emotions that are emanating from within. Try to identify them. What is their intensity? How many are there? Go to this place often, and become conscious of these emotions. Being in tune with them automatically calms them. By bringing these to your awareness, you will be able to identify the highest drives that you have. They are not insane, grasping cries of anguish. Rather, they are calm, certain, strong and pleasant. Listen to your heart. The answers are there. Do not attempt to force the heart into relaxing. That would be nuts. Just be aware of it. Once it feels listened to, it will respond with harmony.

Work from this center. Let go of the pressures of the world. Let go of all you feel that you have to do. Let go of your guilt and your shame. Let go of what you think others want you to feel, think and do. This is illusion. Go to the source of Truth. Go within. This is the easiest thing in the world. Stop what you are doing this instant and relax your mind heart and body. You are under no obligations any longer. See these obligations for what they truly are: Vain imaginings! Release them. They serve you no longer. Relax.

The Will

"If you are still alive today, it is because you have chosen it."

Chapter 11
The Will

There is but one will in the Universe. That is the will to Exist. This is the very reason that the Universe exists. Because it has a will to! The Universe is alive. You are alive as part of this Universe, because you have a will to exist. If you are still alive today, it is because you have chosen it. There is no point in trying to develop your will. You already have one. You must only become aware of it, and be in harmony with it.

Your will to exist manifests itself in two ways: First, as a collective will to co-create, and second, as an individual will for you to be alive. The will to co-create expresses itself most strongly as the will to procreate. This is one of the most powerful forces in the Universe. Rather than tame the urge to reproduce, it is much wiser to harness this enormous power and to bend it to your purposes.

Your individual will to live has two facets. These two are related to your perception of the world. As you perceive the world, you identify things in the world as either beneficial or as harmful to you. In the case of things that you identify as beneficial, you feel attracted to them. In the case of things that you identify as harmful, you feel repulsed by them. Attraction and repulsion are expressions of the unified force of the universe, which can be observed easily in nature in magnets. Magnets can both repulse and attract.

This is the exact same phenomenon. It is not in your imagination. It is real. It is a force of nature that you feel in your emotions in connection with conditions and people in your life. You are a magnet. More than that, you are an electro- magnet. What you are feeling when you feel attraction or repulsion is the electrical energy in your body being expressed as a magnetic force either repelling or attracting the material objects in your world.

These feelings are very important clues for you. Do not discard them. Attraction is often felt as desire and repulsion is often felt as fear. You have often heard people tell you to act despite your fear. I am telling you that this is a very dangerous thing to do. If fear tells you not to do a thing, don't do it. You are not yet ready. Rather, embrace your fear, and understand it. Shine a light in the darkness.

Have you ever tried to make a child face their fear? Let us suppose for example that your child is afraid of dogs. Your child sees a dog, and turns away in fear. What will happen if you force the child to go to the dog? It is unlikely that your child will embrace the dog. More likely, the fight or flight responses of the child will be activated to their highest level, and the kid will freak out and pitch a fit.

Why should you do violence to yourself in this way? Instead, slow down; take the time to feel your emotions and to listen to the messages that your highest self is trying to express to you through them. When you are clear on the message, then you can calmly choose to deal with the situation- or not. Be kind and gentle with yourself. Treat yourself the way that you would like to be treated. If you are not kind to yourself, who will be?

The other facet of your will to live is through attraction and desire. When an image of something that you desire enters your mind, your electro- magnet is switched on. Electrical energy is sent through your body, and outward into the world, and it is palpable. In sexual matters, we call this being "Turned- On". Everyone understands this powerful urge to move towards another. You can feel the energy between people in this state.

Now, understand this: Everything in the world is magnetic. The earth itself is a magnet. Its attractive force is partly expressed as gravity. Every object that has any mass at all, also expresses a gravitational force. Attraction is always mutual. Be very clear on this next statement:

WHAT YOU ARE ATTRACTED TO IS ALSO ATTRACTED TO YOU!

Consider this: When two magnets move towards each other, which one is doing the attracting? Both are! Both magnets attract each other. Now, suppose that one of the magnets is an electro- magnet. While it is dormant, the attractive power is weak. When it is switched on, and another magnet moves towards it, which has done the attracting? They still both have mutually attracted each other. One has initiated the action, but both have moved towards each other.

So it is with your endeavor to become a millionaire. You have turned on your electro-magnet. YOUR MILLION DOLLARS IS ATTRACTED TO YOU AND MOVING TOWARDS YOU! There is no great effort that you must make. Simply feel the power of your desire. Unless you actively interfere with the process, this wealth will manifest itself in your life.

Effortlessness

"If you feel that you are making an effort at something it is because you are doing something out of alignment with your motivation."

Chapter 12
Effortlessness

Effort is an error. If you feel that you are making an effort at something it is because you are doing something out of alignment with your motivation. Effort is something that "They" want you to exert to reach "Their" goals. Who are "They"? Everyone other than you!

At work, they want you to sacrifice your time. The society has millions of tasks for you to do. There is a never-ending reservoir of projects to drain your energy. There is an endless supply of people who will steal a piece of your time and energy.

If you truly wish to do something, then there is no effort involved. It is easier to continue doing it than to stop doing it. Therefore, if you feel that you are exerting an effort, stop and ask yourself if your activity is aligned with your motivation. Listen to your intuition.

Wait until you receive "Inspiration". With an inspiration, you will have an idea of what to do, and this idea will carry its own energy. Certainly it will energize you enough to carry the project through to its completion. You must protect this energy, and use it for its intended purpose, or "They" will find things for you to do with your energy that is not in alignment with your goals, purposes and motivation.

The main tool that "They" use to cause you to divert your energy, and make efforts in the tasks that they want you to perform is shame. If you do not do it, then you are not a team player. You are selfish. You are evil. You do not deserve to be a member of the society. They tell you that your duty is even more important than your life. Do you really believe this to be in your self-interest?

And you react to this, because they attack you where it hurts you most. You want to be a good person. You have always wanted that. You don't understand why "They" still have something against you, even though you tried to do everything that "They" have asked. So you make an effort. You pull out all of your reserve energy and you offer it to "Them".

But they will never have enough. They will never be satisfied. Their demands are infinite. Some of what you have imagined to be their demands are not even real. They exist only in your imagination. You have internalized their demand, have tried to predict them, and have created an idealized version of yourself. You believe that if you are perfectly giving, that you give them all of your energy, that they will give you all the rewards that you desire.

This is where the error lies. You are good enough. You must claim your own rewards. You must do for yourself. You must bring your own desires into your life.

You have chosen to be a millionaire. Do you really believe that by continuing to surrender all of your energy and making all these efforts for them, that they will then hand you a million dollars? What does your experience tell you? What does your intuition tell you? Is it not infinitely more likely that by setting your own goals, and by working towards them in your own way, that in this way you will achieve results that you desire?

The fact is that you are making efforts to please other peoples' insatiable desires. In the process you are depleting your energy reserves. You are diverting your Life-Force away from what you really want. There is only one thing to do: STOP. Wait for inspiration, and then, follow your inspiration, with no detours. You will recognize the right path to your million dollars, because it will be an effortless path, with no demands for which you do not have sufficient energy.

You will be a millionaire when you effortlessly follow your inspiration.

Keep Your Big Mouth Shut

"Don't tell anyone anything. Don't tell them that you intend on being a millionaire, don't tell them about your projects. Don't tell them about your beliefs; don't tell them about your incredible ideas, just keep your big mouth shut!"

Chapter 13
Keep Your Big Mouth Shut

Your voice is like an echo. When you stand and shout in front of a cliff, you will hear an echo. This happens without fail. If you are in a spot where there are echoes, you will hear your own voice reflected to you after a time delay. Sound travels one mile in about five seconds. So, if you are a mile away from the echoing surface, you will hear your voice returned to you in about ten seconds. In the time when you are waiting, do you doubt that you will hear the echo? No. You are certain that it will return to you. And you just wait.

When you stand and ask for your million dollars, there will be a time lag. Think of it as the echo. Have the same faith that you have in the echo. As you will certainly hear your voice, you will certainly obtain the object of your request.

The universe is a simple place. There is only one Universal law. This law is expressed in many different forms, and they are all parallel. The same law that regulates the vibrations of sound you emit to hear an echo, regulates the vibrations of thought that you emit to receive the money you have asked for.

Consider this: The laws of physics have their parallels in the laws of interpersonal relations, personal growth, metaphysics, and the list goes on. There are not many different laws. There is one law expressed differently. All that you have ever obtained in your life has been through this law, and no other. It is impossible to circumvent this law, or to subordinate it to a law of your invention.

In order to receive your million dollars as quickly and effortlessly as possible, you must clear the way for the echo of your vibrations. If there are things between you and your echo, it will be diminished or deadened. That is why you do not hear an echo in the forest: all the trees surrounding you deaden the sound. With sound, you will also have difficulty hearing your echo if there are other sound vibrations interfering. So it is with your thoughts. If there are other thought vibrations interfering with yours, then you will have difficulty manifesting your desire into your material plane.

Other vibrations can come from either your own conflicting thoughts or the thoughts of others. It is work enough to deal with your own conflicting thoughts. You certainly don't need the vibrations of others interfering with your progress.

How do you avoid allowing the thoughts of others to interfere? Simple: KEEP YOUR BIG MOUTH SHUT! Don't tell anyone anything. Don't tell them that you intend on being a millionaire, don't tell them about your projects. Don't tell them about your beliefs; don't tell them about your incredible ideas, just keep your big mouth shut! They may not necessarily have the intention to interfere, but it is absolutely certain that any thought that does not originate from you will divert your thought vibrations.

This takes discipline, and discipline is easy once you realize what your objective is. Your objective is to become a millionaire. Your objective is not to tell everyone. If you have not yet achieved your goal, then there is no need to tell anyone about it. What purpose will it serve? It will only disperse your energy. This energy is much better off being channeled into achieving your objective than having to explain and defend your opinions. They don't need to know what you are up to. If you have achieved your goal, then there is no need to tell anyone, it is obvious that you have succeeded.

If you really feel the need to tell everyone about your projects, then wait until it is realized. Until then, keep your big mouth shut.

Resolve

"You cannot tell yourself that you will do your best. Your best is not good enough. You must DO IT."

Chapter 14
Resolve

There is nothing to stop you from becoming a millionaire. Many people have done it before you, many people will do it after you, and many people are doing it right now. Why not you? The only difference between those who have done it and those who haven't is that the first group has done it. Period. There is no other difference. Those who have done it decided that they were going to do it, and then did whatever it took.

This is the true nature of commitment. When you are truly committed, you will do whatever it takes. You will not tolerate distractions and diversions. Once you have identified your destination, you walk towards it with a sure-footed step. Decisions become easy. You must develop this feeling of commitment. You must place all of your energies on this objective, and then allow all of your energy to direct you to that goal.

But this is a different kind of commitment from what you are used to. This is a firm resolve. An unshakable intention! You cannot tell yourself that you will do your best. Your best is not good enough. You must DO IT. Trying is a myth. There is no such thing as trying to do something. You either do it or you do not. You must not look back. You must not consider any other options. No contingency plans.

You must be completely rational. You must remember the fact that other people have done it. This fact implies that it is possible to do it. This also means that there is a way of doing it. The fact that others have discovered this method also means that it is possible for anyone to discover this method. Any doubts that you have about this are really because you doubt in yourself.

Why should you believe that you could do it? Because you can! How can you know this to be true? Think it through. If others have learned the method for becoming a millionaire, then it can be learned. If others have learned it, then it means that there is a learning mechanism in human beings that is capable of learning this. If others have made their learning system work, then it is possible to make the learning system work for you.

But, why you? Well, simply compare your learning system to the learning systems of successful millionaires. There is no reason why you cannot know what they know. For the most part, you have learned the things that you chose to learn. From learning to walk to learning to read and to write, you have learned. This is also true for millionaires. They have learned most of the same things that you have learned. There are things that you know that they do not know. Your home phone number for example. They don't know that. The energy that you have devoted to learning other things, they have devoted to learning the method for becoming millionaires. Had you devoted an equivalent amount of energy to learning the process, you would have known what they know. You can see clearly now that there is no real difference between you and a millionaire: Only that they have made the choice to become a millionaire.

Once you make this choice, you must not turn back. Each time you devote energy to becoming a millionaire, this new energy is not added to the previous energy, it is multiplied. If you quit and start over later, you will have to build up this energy charge again.

You must make up your mind once and for all, and resolve to do what it takes. Right now, you have no idea what it will take. But as you progress, you will have to match your energy to perceived obstacles, and they will test your resolve. There is nothing that can stop you if your resolve is firm. If you have built up your energy, then vibrations from an obstacle will be weaker than your vibrations, and the perceived obstacle will give way. You must, however, keep your resolve and your faith, which is founded in understanding and certainty. You must not imagine the obstacle to have any power over you. You must refuse to bow to it. You are strong. You must not give in to your fear-induced imagining of your weakness. You are Indestructible. You must not give in to your vain imagined vulnerability. The world is vibration. The strongest vibration is the one that will create your reality. Allow yours to be the strongest. Do not entertain doubt. RESOLVE TO BE A MILLIONAIRE.

Get Over It

"If you are caught up in your grief over minor or major incidents, then you will not achieve anything."

Chapter 15
Get Over It

In order to overcome obstacles, you must become resilient. Resilience is the ability to "Get Over It". Each day, as we move through the world, we are subjected to innumerable small emotional upsets. Sometimes, we are even faced with larger and more major ones. These range from stepping in chewing gum to the death of a loved one. Each time an upsetting event occurs, our defensive systems kick in, to help us heal from the trauma. Healing takes time. Recovery is not instantaneous.

However, you must still continue on with your day, and eat and sleep and work and play, and do all of the other things that you wish to do. If you are caught up in your grief over minor or major incidents, then you will not achieve anything. As you have selected to become a millionaire, you must be able to devote your time and energy to this endeavor, and not live in the past, in your little upsets.

Think of your resilience system in this way: Every morning when you get up out of bed, you are handed a stack of 100 "Resilience Chips" which work like currency. Every time that life hands you an upsetting event, you turn over a certain number of chips. For example, if someone cuts you off on the road, you hand over 1 chip. If your boss chews you out, you hand over 2 chips.

Each person hands over a different number of chips for the same event, since each person perceives the events differently. The number of chips you hand over for a given event is related to how much the event means to you. If you have a tendency to take things with a grain of salt, you will hand over less chips than if you have a tendency to blow everything out of proportion.

Question: Which person is more likely to become a millionaire more rapidly: The person who is resilient or the person who is not?

I ask this obviously rhetorical question to make a point: You must take control of the number of resilience chips that you hand out each day. If you lose all your chips by noon each day, you are wasting the rest of the day incapacitated. If, on the other hand, you go to bed each night with a stack of leftover chips, those chips will be added to your resilience for the next day, and you will begin the day with a head start. You will feel stronger and more invincible.

How do you control the number of chips? In two simple ways: First, take it easy. Stop reacting to everything as a catastrophe. Learn to put things in perspective and take them in stride. Expect that not everything will go your way all the time. Don't get caught up in small, meaningless battles. They are not worth it. Save your chips for a time when they will be really useful. Learn to distinguish between a problem and an inconvenience. A problem is an obstacle that threatens you or your family's health, safety, or well-being. Anything that is not life threatening is simply an inconvenience. Save your chips only for real problems. For all of life's inconveniences, just overlook them. If someone engages you in a senseless confrontation, wave him or her off. If you allow your resilience to be depleted it will affect everything, including your physical energy and your mental processes. You will begin to entertain doubt, and have mental images of failure. Your fears and negative thoughts will enter your mind. You will become preoccupied with potential obstacles to your goal, and your mind will become filled with "what ifs..." If you waste your energy on inconveniences or trying to find solutions to all your "what ifs" before they arise, you will have no more energy to focus on your goal and nothing will ever get done. Don't waste your energy on problems and inconveniences that have not even surfaced yet. Save your chips for real problems and obstacles: There are enough of those.

Second, get some rest. When your chip reserve is depleted, rest restores it. Take a nap, get some sleep, meditate, go sit in a garden. Do whatever you have to do, but just relax. As you get some rest, you will begin to feel a sense of joy well up inside you. This is a sign that your resilience reserves are filling up. Be gentle to yourself, and you will become more robust.

This new approach will allow you to generate the power required to reach your objective of becoming a millionaire. Each day, you will be able to move past the challenges, and come closer to your dream.

Don't Lose Money

"The bottom line is THE BOTTOM LINE. Don't lose money!"

Chapter 16
Don't Lose Money

Consider this. Most people are willing to take a few losses early in the entrepreneurial process. They figure that they will be able to make up for those losses once they increase their sales. This ridiculous approach is the reason why 80% of new enterprises go out belly up in the first two years. If you want to be bankrupt in two years, then go ahead and start losing money now. But this book is about becoming a millionaire, not about becoming broke.

Keep in mind how things work. Once you set a process in motion, it tends to continue. This is momentum. If you start a business by losing money, you are setting up a money losing business. This is quite simple, really. As your money-losing business grows, you will learn to lose more and more money. After some time, your business will have reached its money-losing potential, and you will have no more money to lose. Your business will have reached its maximum loss ability. Congratulations, your business has accomplished what it was set up to do.

On the other hand, if you start making money from day one, it is not possible to lose money. If you never engage in a transaction that loses money, you won't lose money.

Think about it. How could you possibly lose money if you never sell at a loss. If someone offers you a losing proposition, don't take it. Just move on, there are loads of other opportunities out there. The more someone tries to convince you of a deal, the more you can be sure that it is in their interest and not yours to do the deal, so don't get bamboozled.

All this sounds simple. But the fact remains that most new businesses fail, and that this failure is due to people losing money. People lose money for one reason, and one reason only. It is because they spend more than they make. It stands to reason, then, that if you do not spend more than you make, you can't lose money. That's the way it is. You think that you cannot make that mistake, but just think how easy it is. You decide to go into business, so you get some offices, and some phones, and you hire some employees. How much have you sold? You're already in the hole, and you are not even out of the gate. Now you are under the gun. You are working to support your employees, your landlord, and your telephone company representative. You will be lucky if you manage to meet your first month's expenses. Chances are you will have to dip into your own savings to stay on top of your bills.

So, the solution? Don't do it. Don't spend money that you don't have. By all means, spend money once you have it, but don't go out and spend a dime until you have earned two dimes. I can't stress this enough. Spending money that you don't have is so common an error that I am convinced that despite my best efforts, some of you will still go out and spend money before it has come in. If you realize that you are doing this, then stop at once. From this moment, don't ever allow yourself to lose money. If you never incur an expense for which you don't have funds, you can never come up short. You can't lose in the long term if you never lose in the short term. So, the bottom line is THE BOTTOM LINE. Don't Lose money!

Dis-Stress

"Preoccupation is the single biggest problem that is caused by stress."

Chapter 17
Dis- Stress

I have never heard anyone say that they don't have enough stress in their life. I have never heard anyone say: "Gee, you know what I need is more stress in my life." This is because Stress is a condition of life. You are hard wired for stress. No stress, no life!

Here's why: Stress is experienced as nervous tension. This nervous tension is actually electric impulses being sent though your nervous system. This nervous system is made up of electric cables. Each nerve is an electric wire, and small electric pulses sent when your neurons fire from your brain control it.

Have you known anyone who is always really very stressed, no matter what is going on in his or her life? You've probably also known someone who seems hardly stressed out at all, no matter what is going on around them. This is a matter of habit. This habit is physical. Different people are used to feeling different amounts of stress in their daily lives. This stress is an addiction. Having these electric charges in their system is exciting. Have you ever had an electric shock? Exciting, huh?

As an adolescent, I had some friends who would get their kicks by "DOING 120". This consisted of taking two ends of a live wire and touching them to get a shock. No kidding! I learned about this when I was over once and was invited to join in. Hey, I'll try anything once. I don't think I'd do it again, but take my word for it, having that much electricity running through your nervous system is, to say the least, exciting.

Additionally, these same electric charges cause your endocrine system to release hormones into your system, which provide sensations similar to recreational drugs. So, in one sense, if you are addicted to stress, you are a drug addict.

One thing that I noticed, while I had 120 volts running through me, was that my vision was blurred. Furthermore, I couldn't think about anything except the jolt. This is where stress becomes Dis-Stress, and can interfere with becoming a millionaire. You can't think about anything but the source of your stress.

This is where people make the most common mistake regarding stress. Most people believe that stress is a reaction to external forces: Stimulus first, then stress. This is completely backwards, and this view will prevent you from dealing with the stress, so that you can devote your energy to becoming a millionaire.

Actually, you have a potential or "Voltage" for stress, that exists whether there is a stressor or not. Similarly, a live wire in your kitchen has a potential of 120 Volts, regardless of whether it is plugged into a microwave, a blender, or nothing at all. What happens to most people is that as soon as one stressor is removed, they plug themselves into another stressor. That way, as one stressor disappears, another one replaces it immediately and they are always stressed about something. Even though that "something" is changing continuously, they maintain a consistent level of stress in their lives. But they are too preoccupied by their stressor to realize this.

Preoccupation is the single biggest problem that is caused by stress. You become preoccupied with whatever your current stressor is, and cannot devote any attention to the process of becoming a millionaire. This is because you cannot hold two distinct thoughts in your mind at one time any more than you can play two movies on the same screen.

You must choose the films that you want to play on the screen of your mind. In order to do this, you must disconnect yourself from the stressors that you have chosen. You must first realize that you were stressed out first, and then you attached your feeling of stress to a stressor around you, whatever it happened to be. It did not cause your stress.

Once you let go of the stressor, and realize that it was not such a big deal, you will temporarily feel a relief, and a sense of well-being, and a brief feeling of freedom. During this time interval, you can choose to attach your emotional electric energy towards achieving your goal of becoming a millionaire.

Whenever feelings of stress return, realize that the stressor does not cause them. Separate them from that stressor and let it go. Then turn your nervous electric energy once again towards becoming a millionaire.

The Fundamental Principle

"To be a Self-made Millionaire, You must be a Self-Made Person."

Chapter 18
The Fundamental principle

So, you want to be a millionaire. Good, we can make that happen for you without a lot of difficulty. Here's how:

Most people will tell you that the way to become a millionaire is by investing wisely in stocks and mutual funds, and investments of that nature. This is a very successful method, which has a lot of merit. However, there is something lacking. That something is time. Through prudent investing, you will get undoubtedly become very wealthy, but it may take the rest of your life. You will get to be the richest person in the cemetery. Congratulations. However, if you want to make a fortune while you still have time to enjoy it, you will have to choose a different tack.

Almost everyone who has become a millionaire within a year is a self-made millionaire. What does that mean exactly? A self-made millionaire is one who has bet on him or herself. When you invest in stocks, you are actually buying a lottery ticket betting on the manager of a company that you may know very little about. This is a lot like betting at the track. You take odds on a horse, given some public information, and you place your bets. How much do you really know about the management on which you are betting?

The system is set up in a way that you must bet blind. If you know more about a certain horse than the other bettors, that is called: "Betting on a tip". If you know more than other bettors about the manager that you are betting on, that is called: "Insider trading", and it is illegal. This is like casino betting. The house always keeps an advantage. According to the laws of probabilities, they must win in the long term. I read somewhere that 80% of people trading in the stock market actually lose money?

Investment professionals talk about diversified portfolios, and not putting your eggs all in one basket. The entrepreneur, on the other hand, puts all her eggs in one basket, her own, and then watches that basket very carefully. Wouldn't you rather bet on a manager that you know everything about and that you trust implicitly? Well, that manager is you, and only you. You can never know as much about anyone else. So, entrepreneurs bet on themselves. And this is the difference. If you bet on yourself, you can't lose, you either make money or you have paid tuition, and as we shall see later on, the tuition fees really aren't as high as you may think.

Thus, in order to become a millionaire this year, you must accept the fact that you are an entrepreneur. The main rule of entrepreneurship is the same as the main rule for investors. Investors will tell you that the way to make money is to buy low and sell high. Sounds simple enough. But the problem is that you do not control what the market is doing. And if you do try to control the market, you go to jail.

Entrepreneurs, on the other hand, have much more control. They do not have to sit around and wait and watch. They are proactive, while investors are reactive. You can't really be a self-made anything unless you are proactive.

Look, as an entrepreneur, you can become a millionaire in one easy step, and here it is: Think of the fundamental rule of entrepreneurship this way: not just "Buy Low, Sell High", but "Buy for a dollar, Sell for Two" it couldn't be any simpler, really. If you want to be a millionaire tomorrow, buy for one million, and sell for two million. Put the difference in your pocket, and you are a millionaire.

Now, I hear you grumbling that if you had a million dollars to invest in a transaction, then you would already be a millionaire. Well, I am going to explain very clearly and simply how you can put those million dollars in your pocket in less than 12 months, doing very little work. The fact is that there are some very simple things that you can do to accumulate the necessary capital.

The essential rule for you to remember here is this: Buy for a dollar, sell for two. As we said, if you were to sell for two million, following this rule, you would have a million dollars in profit. Is this possible? You bet. You could, for example, buy a foreclosed income property for one million that is worth two million. Real estate investors do this every day. You could also buy inventory from a bankruptcy, and sell it at a fair market value. Other entrepreneurs also do this every day. You could buy one large lot of, say, Coca-Cola or whatever, and sell that for twice what you paid.

The Dialogue

"Does the butterfly do anything inside the cocoon? "

So, how do I become a millionaire?

Yes, that's all very nice, but you haven't told me *do!*

Ok, but what do I do exactly?
exactly

Ok. But we still haven't done anything.

Fine, but when are we going to take action?

"Just get up and start, and then don't stop until you're done."

Chapter 20
The plan

OK, here it is: The plan! This is the shortest chapter in the book. I don't want you to get caught up in details; I want you out there working on your project, so that you can be a millionaire this year.

1. Identify something that someone wants, find out what they want to pay.
2. Go looking for this item or service for half the offering price
3. Once you find it, contact both the buyer and seller.
4. Make the deal.
5. Using that money, repeat steps 1 through 4*
    *If you start with $1,000, repeat this 10 times.
    *If you start with $1, repeat this 20 times.

Now, what kind of person are you? Are you the kind of person who is looking for flaws in my system, or are you the kind of person to take action? This system is as simple as it gets. If you are looking for complexity, you will get lost in it. You choose! You can make results or you can make excuses, but you can't do both. I have given you every ounce of effort that I can, the rest is up to you

The New Beginning

"Unwavering decision. This is the alpha and the omega."

Epilogue
The New Beginning

Unwavering decision. This is the alpha and the omega. This is the beginning and the end. You decide. You do what you know to be right. Thus far in the book, you have listened to what I have had to say, and I thank you for your attention. Now I will make the most shocking statement in this book: I AM WRONG!

How can this be? No author has ever declared himself or herself to be in error! It is against the unwritten code of authors and intellectuals! Well, what I have expressed here is my truth. And it is true for me alone. Your truth may be similar on many points, and it may differ significantly on others. I encourage you to discover for yourself your own inner guide of truth. Your moral guide lies within you. Your instructions for creating wealth lie inside of you, not of me.

My intention here has not been to substitute myself as your oracle in place of the social conditioning that you have received. My intention has been to break you of your social conditioning in order to return you to yourself and to "Return you to your senses" as it were. This means that from here on in, it's your life; you are to go into yourself for guidance, and not to me or to anyone else. The events of your life have caused you to shut off your higher "senses." they have caused you to doubt yourself and what you know to be true. I have no interest in keeping you deluded. Society, however, does have an interest in dulling your senses and keeping you shackled as a "Productive consumer." I doubt that this was your childhood dream. I don't think that you said to yourself that you would one day be a productive consumer. Break free.

For this reason, I have avoided giving specific tactics for wealth creation in this volume. I don't want you following my path, or any path that I create. It may not be right for you, and would certainly weaken your self-reliance. Further, it would turn me into some sort of guru, which I have no interest in becoming. I am no more infallible than you are. I would like to deal with the strongest part of people, not the weakest, the most self-affirming, not the most dependent. What would make me happy is finding out that every reader has discovered his own path and followed it, and has achieved the wealth that they chose.

Contact
Call me what you will, just call me...

You may very well ask: what's in it for me? Why do I care to help people to become millionaires? Simple. The more people that become rich through my influence, the more the vibrations in the universe create abundance for me. Pretty neat, huh?

Ok, so the universe is a simple place. It is all just vibration, and these vibrations are under our direct control. Vibrations begin in the mind and then get amplified through the mechanisms of the universe. And there are simple ways to amplify the vibrations that we create in the universe.

One of the simplest ways for you to increase your vibrations of wealth is to wish what you want for yourself for others. If you wish happiness for yourself, wish it for others. In this way you multiply the vibrations of that experience in your environment. There's only one of you, but there are six billion people in the world. Wishing happiness for all multiplies your vibrations six billion times.

In your case, if you wish for millions of dollars to manifest into your environment, the best thing to do is to help others manifest the same thing into their environment. The more you do this and the more completely you do this, the more wealth you will manifest into your life with effortless ease. Not bad. You can do this by providing tools and inspiration to others.

If you would like to share the tools and inspiration of E-Motion with others through this book, or would like to order additional copies for yourself, I would be happy to provide you with special pricing for any orders, as it is in both our interests to propagate the knowledge contained in E-Motion to the world. The more we create abundance for others using this method, the more abundant vibrations we will create for ourselves. Everybody wins!

If you have any success stories, let me know. I will be happy to hear from you!

God Bless,
John R. Colt

John R. Colt is available for **Keynotes** and **Seminars, as well as private consulting**

Suite #101
470 Harris
Saint Laurent, QC
H4N 2H3 Canada

Discounts available for volume orders!

Printed in the United States
3980